101 TS

TO DO WITH YOUR

CHRISTMAS

ELF

JASON DEAS

Racehorse Publishing

Racehorse Publishing books may be purchased in bulk at special discounts for sales promotion, corporate gifts, fund-raising, or educational purposes. Special editions can also be created to specifications. For details, contact the Special Sales Department, Skyhorse Publishing, 307 West 36th Street, 11th Floor, New York, NY 10018 or info@skyhorsepublishing.com.

Racehorse for Young Readers™ is a pending trademark of Skyhorse Publishing, Inc.®, a Delaware corporation.

Visit our website at www.skyhorsepublishing.com.

10 9 8 7 6 5 4 3 2 1

Library of Congress Cataloging-in-Publication Data is available on file.

Cover design by Michael Short

Cover photograph by Jason Deas
Interior photography by Jason Deas

ISBN: 978-1-944686-62-8
eISBN: 978-1-944686-63-5

Printed in China

This book is dedicated to magic. To not knowing. To a full imagination.

It's also dedicated to my wife, kids, and knowing.

May all your days, in every season, be merry and bright.

Table of Contents

Introduction

I was introduced to the world of elves a few years ago by my sister's children. Thanks a lot, kids! I have to admit that at first it seemed like a bit of a chore to do something special with the elf every night. However, I have seen the joy it brings my own children and decided a few years ago to take on the task full force. I realized we didn't have very many more years of Christmas magic at our house and I wanted to be able to look back on these years with delight, knowing I did everything in my power to keep the magic alive.

I think the first thing you have to decide when you get an elf is what type of elf you have. Is the elf mischievous? Is the elf a troublemaker? Or is he fun-loving? Do you have one elf for each kid or do they share one? We have nine. And yes, I need professional help. All of my ideas will work with one elf or nine. Don't worry—I'm going to make your holiday merry and bright. Kick back with a cup of eggnog and enjoy.

Some friends of mine have a naughty elf who makes a mess in their house. We don't have those sorts of elves in our house, so you won't find any of those ideas in this guide. It is easy to make a mess—I am sure most people can figure that out on their own.

Some elves hide. We did this for a couple years. Now that the kids are a little older they know all our spots, and, quite honestly, they don't have much time in the morning before school to play hide-and-seek. If you're ever in a jam and don't have much time, it's always a possibility. I use it once or twice during the season.

We have plush elves that the kids are allowed to touch and play with. We set them on the fireplace at bedtime so they can fly home to help Santa make toys, and then they're back in the morning. Our elves don't spy or tattle. Like I said, our elves are all about fun and the joy of the season.

Our elves are playful and have great imaginations. Some mornings the kids might come downstairs to find them "sunning" on beach towels with bottles of suntan lotion beside them. They'll have on sunglasses and swimming

goggles. Maybe a raft or boogie board by their side.

It's all about creating a scene. My children love it and I hope yours will, too.

Pretend you are decorating a department store window. A little imagination goes a long way. An elf sitting under an umbrella with some balled-up, blue copy paper and a few blue streamers hanging from the ceiling fan or the umbrella is easily transformed through the eyes of a child.

Most of the things I use are found around the house or come from dollar variety stores. I probably spend less than two dollars a night, and most nights I spend nothing at all. For sixty dollars (give or take) I can fill my children's heads with memories to last a lifetime. I have provided a list of items I have used the most.

Within this book, I provide additional ways you can embellish and add onto my idea and make them your own! I'm sure your closets, garages, and basements are filled with many little treasures to create amazing scenes for your elf.

Have fun with it. Don't feel like you have to do it like everybody else. Make your own rules for what works with your life. With a little bit of pre-planning and scouting around the house for stuff, it'll be awesome. Remember to see it through the eyes of a child. Merry Christmas!

Elf Shopping List

- Painter's tape
- Yarn (red and yellow)
- Marshmallows (small and large)
- One piece of poster board
- Toothpicks
- Copy paper (white and blue)

- Balloons (assorted colors)
- Tissue paper
- Buffalo snow or cotton balls
- Pipe Cleaners
- Easter grass
- Streamers (blue and white)

Disclaimer: Some scenarios contain small parts and other potential hazards for children, if left unsupervised by an adult. Please take all necessary precautions and do not leave children unattended around scenes.

The Slide

Find anything in the house you can make a slide with, and possibly something for the elf to ride down on. I used a simple ironing board and a tiny float I found in the garage. I propped the ironing board on our piano bench, positioned the elf, and voila! It took me about five minutes. From my children's reaction, you would have thought it took me hours.

If you don't have an ironing board, you can use a piece of wood, a big piece of cardboard, a baby bed mattress, the leaf from the dining room table that you never use, or anything to create the illusion of a slide.

If you don't have a float, a laundry basket could work, or the elf can just slide on its own. Sometimes, I put the elf on the float and place other stuffed animals in different poses at different points on the slide so it looks like they're all having fun together.

All of these ideas will work for just one elf, but will be a lot more fun with additional friends. So, go out and buy more elves! Or you can always use teddy bears, dolls, and other stuffed animals as extras.

Supplies:

- Ironing board (or something similar) to make slide
- Bench or chair to prop slide
- Float or other small item for elf to ride (optional)

Mechanical Breakdown

I will readily admit that when it comes to car engines, I am completely lost. When I open the hood of a car, I might as well be staring into the abyss or the eyes of a spaghetti monster.

If you have kids, I'm sure you have some sort of large toy car, dump truck, tractor, or other vehicle laying around that your elf can fix. If you happened to have a toy sleigh, that would be even better. Prop the vehicle up, lay your elf underneath, and place a couple tools scattered around so it looks like she's making some repairs.

Supplies:

- Toy vehicle
- A scattering of random tools
- Two items to prop the vehicle

Ping-Pong Champ

I love ping-pong. I'm no professional, but I am the family champion. Or I was, until my nephew grew up. Now you can make your elf a ping-pong champion.

I set this one up on the kitchen table. You can use the counter or the floor just as easily. I used streamers as a net taped to heavy glasses. A couple of ping-pong paddles and ping-pong balls will have your elf set up in a creative scene and you in bed tonight without breaking a sweat.

Supplies:

- Ping-pong paddles and balls
- Streamer or similar item to make a net
- Glasses (to support the net)

Rainy Day

I know most elves are used to snow, so throw the kids a curve and give them a rainy day. I bought a roll of blue streamers and had some sky blue construction paper around the house, which I cut and balled up to create makeshift paper raindrops. I even found a box of Easter supplies and grabbed some blue Easter grass from one of the baskets to sprinkle around. I grabbed an umbrella, set the elves underneath with the raindrops scattered around, and taped a few pieces of the blue streamer coming down from the umbrella.

You can make this one even more convincing if you hang more streamers from the ceiling or a ceiling fan. You can even turn the ceiling fan on low to simulate a hurricane. Rain boots might also be cute.

If you want to get really crazy and happen to have a sound machine or sound app on your phone, you can add another auditory element to your scene. Just set it up, turn on the rain or thunderstorm setting, and you've added a whole new dimension to your work.

Supplies:

- Umbrella
- Blue streamer
- Blue copy paper
- Extra credit: blue Easter grass
- Sound machine (optional)

Airplane Madness

This scenario is another one that will get a great reaction from the kids. It takes some planning and about thirty minutes of prep time, but it's worth it. If you don't know how to make a paper airplane, get someone to teach you a simple design or consult the Internet.

After the children go to bed, fold anywhere from ten to fifty paper airplanes and place them in the tree, on the mantle, and scattered in other places around the room. We had so many we even put them between couch cushions, on the kitchen counter, and all over the floor.

Then set up your elf on the fireplace mantle—or on another high vantage point in your living room—with airplanes under his arms and in his lap to make it appear as if he had climbed up there to throw them.

This is an easy clean-up. If you have time, ball the paper up, put it in a trash bag, and save for later.

Supplies:

- Copy paper
- Paper airplane design (use your favorite search engine)
- Extra time (twenty to thirty minutes of preparation)

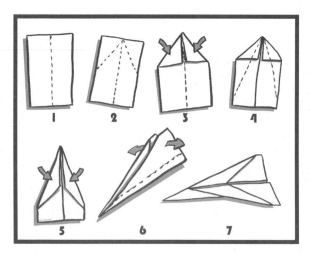

Watch the Birdy

I was in the garage one afternoon and found a pair of binoculars. I quickly envisioned a bird-watching scene, where the elf would be holding the binoculars and looking out the window, but I didn't have time on this particular night to figure out how to make the elf hold the binoculars. I also wanted to sprinkle birdseed around the scene, but preferred to stay out of trouble with Mrs. Deas.

For this scene, you can even make paper birds and hang them outside the window. Set your elf up so that it appears as if he or she is bird watching. There's tons of ways to get creative with this one.

Supplies:

- Binoculars
- Bird seeds (optional)
- Construction paper to create paper birds (optional)

Oven Door Surprise

The membership club near my house sells these enormous muffins, and on rare occasions, I cave in and buy a pack. Carrying these things to the car gave me some indication of their nutritional value; my arms were sore by the time I got across the parking lot. I thought, I can make the elf a baker!

I told Mrs. Deas we had to get them for this setup and she eyed me suspiciously. (Luckily, she likes them too and let it slide.) For this one, I open the oven door and placed a bag of flour, the elf, a whisk, and, of course, the muffins. Hurray, muffins.

Supplies:

- Muffins
- Whisk
- Mixing bowl
- Flour, sugar, and other baking ingredients

Baby, Baby

Hopefully you still have some baby stuff around the house. Let's make the elf look like a baby! A pacifier, a rattle, a blanket. Maybe put the elf in a stroller or baby bed. It doesn't get much simpler than that. And this baby won't wake you up in the middle of the night for a feeding or to change a dirty diaper!

Supplies:

- Baby items such as a pacifier, rattle, bib, burp rag, diaper, bottle, etc.
- Extra credit: stroller, pack-n-play, crib

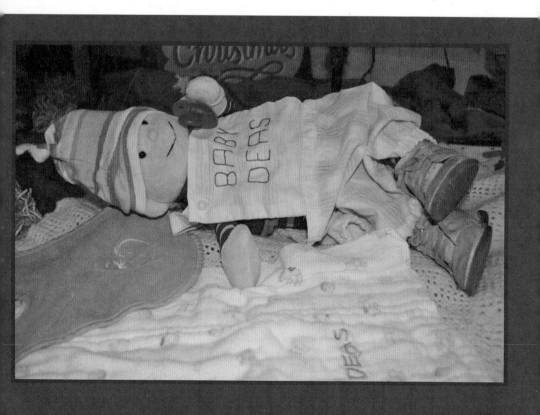

Road Trip

Who doesn't love a good road trip?

Your elf should be able to experience life on the road, too! For this scene, I used a big toy Jeep and filled it with my elf and a friend. After that, I added a map, two pieces of beef jerky, and an old GPS I had in the garage.

The kids had the beef jerky for breakfast. I'm such a good dad.

Supplies:

- Large toy vehicle
- Snacks, map, GPS device (optional)

Beauty Shop

Get out your brushes, scissors, hair dryers, gels, sprays, and other hair potions to create this scene. You can even cut a few pieces of yellow or brown yarn and place them on the floor to make it appear as if the elf got a haircut. This might be a bad option if you have younger kids who might try to reenact this later. Use your judgment.

Supplies:

- Hair supplies (such as hair spray, gel, mousse, brush, etc.)
- Scissors
- Yarn

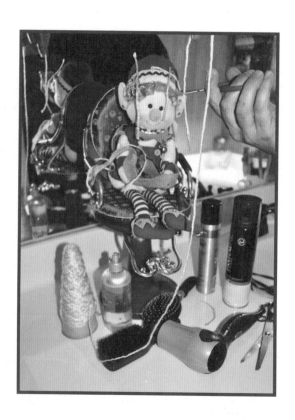

Bubble Gum

This scene is one of my favorites, and it's very easy to set up. Place gum and gum wrappers around your elf, and then blow up a giant pink balloon, as if your elf is blowing a bubble. I also added a stuffed animal friend. I had to tape part of the balloon to the back of the monkey's face to make it stay in place. I was able to wedge the balloon between the elf's face and the tree after a few attempts to stabilize it.

Supplies:

- Pink balloons
- Tape
- Bubble Gum

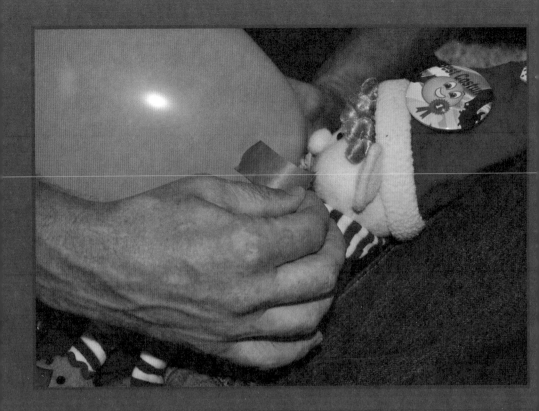

Mr. Clean Up

Elves may not be known for cleaning up, but I still made it look like ours were trying. I used a dustpan and a handheld broom, a couple bottles of cleaning spray, and a few other things to complete the scene. I even added a garbage bag that was supposed to look like the elf was taking out the trash. The kids thought the bag was a surprise full of gifts the elf had brought them, and were surprised when they ripped it open only to find trash. You may want to leave the bag of trash out of your scene.

Supplies:

- Cleaning supplies such as sprays, paper towels, or trash bags
- Cleaning tools such as a broom, mop, or duster

Your Inner Bob Ross

I hope you know who Bob Ross is. If not, your life is not complete and you should take a YouTube break. He was a well-known painter and the television host of *The Joy of Painting*.

This scene is another easy one. With a little planning, you can get this stuff ready during the day and just place your pieces around the elves after the little ones are tucked into bed and have sugarplums dancing in their heads.

I cut out shapes from construction paper to make a train. Additionally, I put some scraps around the elves, a bottle of glue, a black crayon, and some tape. I have to say, the kids were impressed with the elves' artistic abilities.

If you're not up for making a train, I'm sure you can draw three circles. Get a black sheet of construction paper and a white crayon and draw a snowman, which consists of three white circles stacked on top of one another—one small, one medium, and one large. Add a carrot nose with an orange crayon (a triangle) and some stick arms with a brown crayon and guess what? You rule! Bob Ross would be so proud.

Supplies:

- Art Supplies (such as scissors, glue, markers, crayons, paper, etc.)

Lame Excuse for a Snowman

The concept here was simple: Buy a few different size marshmallows and some toothpicks. I put the bigger marshmallows on the bottom and added smaller ones as I built up. I imagined a wondrous snowman.

What I got was an alien white blob. At least you can eat the marshmallows afterward.

Supplies:

- Different size marshmallows
- Toothpicks

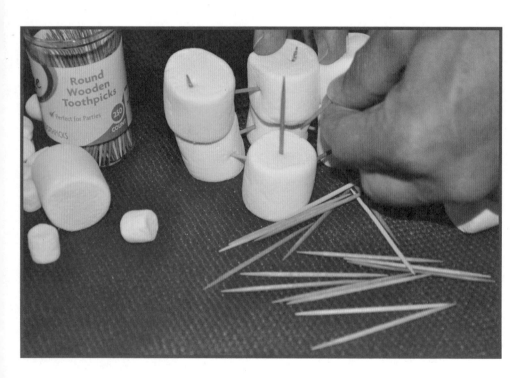

Marshmallow Roast

I hope your snowman from the last scenario looked better than mine. I'm sure it did! If you already have marshmallows, all you need now are a few sticks. Remember, if you only have one elf, you can always use teddy bears, dolls, and other stuffed animals to make it look like more of a party.

My original plan was to place the marshmallows on the ends of the sticks, lean them into the fireplace, and call it a night, but Mrs. Deas wanted to add a layer of authenticity to the scene by actually roasting some of the marshmallows. At least that's what she said her reasoning was—until she started eating all the props and the real reason was revealed to me. Roasted marshmallows are delicious!

Turn on the fan to prevent the sweet, smoky aroma from waking the kids!

Supplies:

- Marshmallows
- Sticks (or toothpicks or thin pretzel rods)

Indoor Swing

Growing up, I remember I always wanted an in-room hammock. I kept telling my dad how easy it would be to attach it to two walls and presto!—I would have an indoor swing. He did buy a hammock, but put it in our yard. I was not amused. That was too easy, and it wasn't in my room.

So, I made our elf an indoor swing with a paper towel roll, yarn, and two pushpins. At least somebody got an indoor swing.

Supplies:

- Paper towel roll
- Yarn or string
- Pushpins

The Beat Goes On

Do you have one of those obnoxious boom boxes in your basement or attic that's as big as a fish tank and takes eighteen D batteries? I still listen to my cassette collection with mine. I haven't counted, but I bet I have three hundred cassettes. I even have those cool holders where you pull out the drawers and each drawer holds ten to twelve cases. They have faux wood and everything. Very classy.

I set the elf on top of the boom box with headphones. I placed some CDs around because my children would have had no idea what the cassettes were.

Supplies:

- Portable radio
- Headphones
- CDs

Jungle

When I take up a hobby, I don't dip my toe into the water, I dive in head first. When I got into houseplants, I didn't just buy two or three, I made it to about forty before Mrs. Deas finally told me to cool my jets. She said if she wanted to live in a jungle, she would move to one.

While I no longer have a jungle of plants, I still have a good number and had the great idea of creating a jungle with them. After the kids went to sleep, I gathered a bunch of the plants together and collected some of my kids' stuffed animals that resemble those one might find in a jungle and created the scene.

Supplies:

- House plants
- Stuffed animals

Million-Dollar Swing

If you have any baseball equipment, it's easy to set up a game for your elves. Use pillows as bases. You're definitely going to need a cast of characters for this one. Gather as many stuffed animals as you can and place them in the positions. Extras can be in the dugout on the opposing team or fans. Gloves, bats, and other props make it even better, so whatever you have, get it out and place it around the scene. I even included one of my trophies.

Supplies:

- Baseball bat, glove, ball, etc.
- Hats
- Pillows or something similar to use as bases
- Stuffed animals
- Trophy (optional)

Snow Day

It's easy to make paper snowflakes. Start with a square, circle, or rectangular piece of paper. Fold the paper in half at least two times. Draw geometric and organic shapes around the outside and cut. After all cuts are complete and the cut pieces have been removed, carefully unfold the paper to reveal your design.

Make ten or so and hang them directly from the ceiling, or from a ceiling fan with yarn, fishing line, or white streamers. Place the elf underneath and maybe a few stuffed animals. If you want to get creative, dress them up in winter clothes or add a sled or other winter toys. You can ball up pieces of paper and add those around the scene to simulate snow.

Supplies:

- Copy paper
- White streamer, fishing line, or white yarn
- Snowflake design (use your favorite search engine—they're simple and quick)

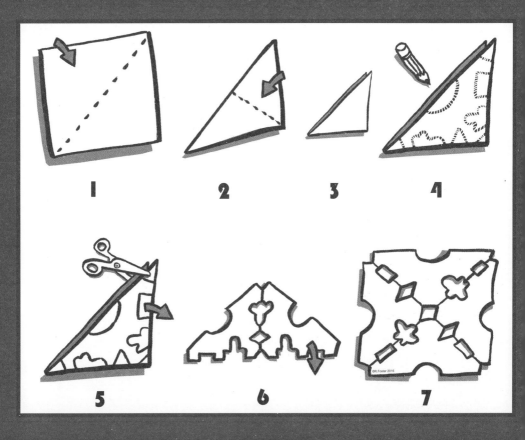

Green Thumb

I used one of our biggest houseplants for this scene. I put down pieces of brown tissue paper in the plant so the elf wouldn't get dirty. Then I set some of my gardening tools around and placed some small peppers we had in the fridge on the paper. You can use carrots as well if you have them. I also set a few sweet potatoes, regular potatoes, and onions in the back of the scene. If you don't have a big plant, this should work fine with even the smallest of house plants or simply placing it on the floor.

Supplies:

- Large house plant (optional)
- Gardening tools
- Vegetables
- Tissue paper

Catching Bugs

I'm in awe of entomologists. What makes a person decide to devote their lives to studying insects? Catching lightning bugs was fun as a kid, but I never thought of making a career out of it. When I was trying to come up with some of my elf ideas, I wandered the aisles of the local dollar store. On one such trip, I found a pack of fake insects for less than a dollar. I'll bet you'll find something similar at your local store if you look. I knew we already had butterfly nets at home and this one was almost too easy. To add another level to the scene, you can print out butterflies, dragonflies, and lightning bugs, and tape them to the wall behind the elf.

Supplies:

- Fake insects
- Butterfly nets and/or flyswatter

Gems and Jewels

I'll admit that I'm not a fan of jewelry. My wife, however, loves it. Here's an opportunity to add some bling to your elf. However, be careful! If you knot up one of your significant other's necklaces, it'll take you the entire weekend to untangle that mess.

Supplies:

- Jewelry

Hanging Out

This one is so easy I felt guilty. I still fell asleep within minutes after finishing setting it up, so I must have not felt too bad. I placed the elf on the top of the ceiling fan blades along with some friends. It's funny how some of the easy ones get the best reactions. The kids loved it when we turned on the fan to shake them off!

Supplies:

- Ceiling fan
- Stuffed animals

I Could Still Rock

My children love music and we've collected a lot of noise-making, I mean, musical instruments through the years. Set up your elf with a few stuffed animal friends and all the musical instruments you can find. Keyboards, tambourines, guitars, kazoos, etc. Rock on.

Supplies:

- Various musical instruments

Outside Looking In

One day I went down into my basement to admire my collection of random items. There, I stumbled upon some wreath holders, which are suction cups with a hook embedded in them.

When I saw the suction cups, I immediately thought of our elf. I suddenly had the idea of sticking her outside the door to our porch. The kids eat breakfast by the window, there was no way they could miss her. Right before they made their daily entrance, I gave the suction cups a good lick, stuck them to the outside of the door, and wrapped the elf's hands to them with pipe cleaners. It took about two minutes.

If you don't have suctions cups with hooks sticking out, which I'd be willing to bet you don't, it will work with push pins and pipe cleaners or yarn. Using these materials won't make a noticeable hole and the elf only has to hang for a few minutes. Depending on your house, you might use a window. If you only have a glass door with no wood to embed the push pins, check out the next idea and improvise with painter's tape.

Supplies:

- Pipe cleaners or yarn
- Push pins or suction cups

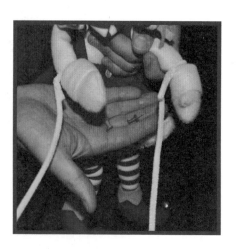

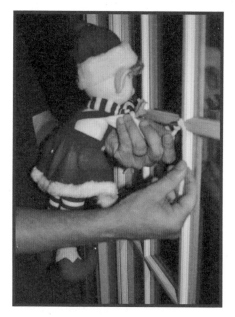

Pretend It's Your Boss

Luckily, I like my boss, but I'm sure some of you may feel differently. For this one, I'm going to think of one of my coworkers. It's been a long day, you forgot your lunch and didn't have time to run out, and somebody said something to you that you just can't get out of your head.

Tape the elf to the wall. Tape him to the ceiling, or tape him any other place that lets you blow off all that negative steam. Tape him upside down or sideways, using the whole roll of tape if you have to. When you are finished, let it go, move on, and have the sweetest dreams, ready to start anew tomorrow. Your kids will love this elf stuff and you are amazing for doing it. The memories will be with them forever. Goodnight.

Supplies:

- Painter's tape

Snack Time

This one takes about two seconds if you have a pet. If you don't have a pet, don't worry. I've got you covered.

If you have a pet, set your elf next to their food bowl. Sprinkle a few pieces of the food on the elf's lap and make the scene even more hilarious by adding a spoon and a fork.

If you don't have any pets, you position the elf as if he or she is eating something odd like uncooked macaroni or spaghetti, a banana peel, a pile of balled up napkins, beads, pennies . . . You get the idea. Look around and you'll find the perfect prop.

Supplies:

- Pet dish and water bowl
- Fork, spoon, straw, etc.

Let's Party

In my college days, I lived in a house built about three feet from a rural highway. Directly across the street was an empty billboard. The bottom of the billboard stood about eight feet off the ground. In my short time in the house, it never held a sign of any kind. It was just an empty box and lonely for some company. So one Friday afternoon a few friends came over and we all had refreshments. After a few rounds of refreshments, someone suggested we climb up in the billboard and wave to cars as they passed. I thought it was a great idea. Somebody else suggested we make it even more entertaining for the passing motorists by putting lampshades on our heads. I thought that was an even better idea. And we did.

As I was searching for an elf idea one night, my eyes fell on the lamp shades in our living room and the memory flashed in the billboard of my mind. So I started removing the lamp shades and placing them on the elf and a few of his friends. This one may have been more for me than for the kids, but they thought it was silly and they were right. It was just as silly twenty something years ago as it is now.

Supplies:

- Lamp shades
- Stuffed animals

Corn Hole

I'm not sure how many of you will know the game corn hole, but if you do, this is about as simple as they come. Set the stage as if the elf is playing against another stuffed animal. Put one of the animals down in a hole for a splash of humor. If you don't know what corn hole is, now would be a good time to find out and order a set. It's good backyard, campground, beach, or lakeside fun. Stores and online retailers also sell miniature sets, which are perfect for this scene.

Supplies:

- Miniature corn hole game

Let's Go To the Movies

I was looking around in the pantry, as I tend to do at about eight o'clock every night. (I know, bad habit.) During my search, I spied a bag of popcorn, which had been in the pantry for a long time. We bought the off brand and regretted our mistake. But it turned out okay as I had my starting point for my elf idea. It was movie night!

If you don't have much time, this is for you. Get some cases from your children's DVDs and Blu-rays and some snacks. Gather all the remote controls. Place the elf in front of the television. I didn't have the movie on when the kids came down but you can do that for extra credit. My kids just assumed the elf had turned it off when they heard them coming.

Tip: Don't use microwave popcorn if your kids are light sleepers or wake up a lot during the night. Microwave popcorn could stink up the Empire State Building.

Supplies:

- Popcorn
- Remote controls
- Movie cases

On Dasher, On Dancer, and Snuggly Dog

You can construct this sleigh ride in less than ten minutes. The difficult part is sneaking all the stuffed animals you'll need out of the children's rooms. I only tripped and fell onto my son's bed once.

I used the same float from the slide scenario as my sled. I set the elf on the sled and lined the animals up in front, two by two. We just so happened to have a reindeer, which I positioned in the front.

We also found a role of ribbon around one of the elf's hands, wrapped it around all the stuffed animals, and tied the ribbon again on the elf's other hand.

Supplies:

- Something to use as sleigh such as small float or pillow
- Ribbon, yarn, or string
- Stuffed animals

Record Player Ride

I might be showing my age here, but I'm not ashamed to say I grew up on records. Do you have a record player stuffed into a corner of the basement or surrounded by cobwebs in the attic? Break it out and leave yourself a little extra time to slap on one of your old records and dance around the living room. This scene will only take a moment or two to assemble.

Set the record player in front of the fireplace or on a low end table so the kids will easily be able to see it. I'm sure there are many ways to do this, but secure the elf with painter's tape so he won't fall off and set the record player on the lowest speed to avoid a casualty. Turn the player on just as the kids are coming down the stairs.

Supplies:

- Record player
- Painter's tape

Cotton Ball Beard

Place the elf in front of the mirror with a razor by his side. (Make sure the guard is on your razor.) I made a cotton ball beard for our elf. It didn't take long. I glued it to a piece of cut poster board and rested it on his lap, so as not to ruin the material on the elf. I'm sure you can use something thin like copy paper as well. I sprayed shaving cream by the elf's side and placed the can next to him to add to the scene. I cut little pieces of yarn in the sink to look like beard hairs.

Supplies:

- Razor and shaving cream
- Cotton balls
- Glue
- Small piece of poster board or sturdy paper

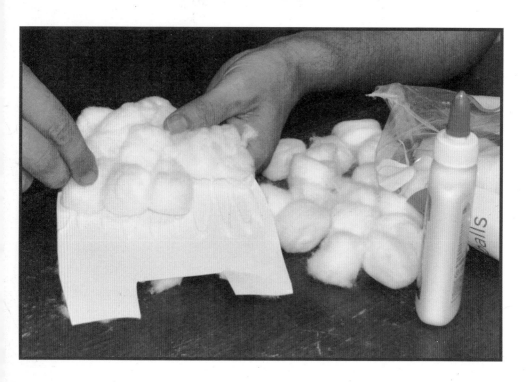

Fun in the Sun

Is it cold at your house? Are you missing summer? Break out all your summer stuff and let's create a summer scene with the elf. For this one, you might use swimming goggles, suntan lotion, rafts and floats, beach towels, sunglasses, and anything you have for the pool or the beach.

Cut a piece of butcher paper with curved edges to look like a pool or lake, then put a raft in the center of it with the elf kicking back and enjoying a relaxing day in the sun with some of her friends. Put sunglasses on some of them. On others, put goggles. Next to the water, I put two beach towels with two more friends with sunglasses and lotion.

Supplies:

- Raft or other pool/beach toys
- Beach items such as sunglasses, sunscreen, goggles

Present Train

Choo! Choo! Here comes the present train. If you had a long day and just can't wait to get into bed and forget the day, this one is for you. It will only take about a minute.

Have you wrapped a few presents? I hope so, because this one uses presents from under your tree. Take some presents and make a curvy line. Set the elf and some friends on top of them as if they were riding in train cars. We just happened to have a train conductor hat on hand, so I slapped that on the one in front and headed off to bed.

And that's that. One minute flat. Brush your teeth and go to sleep!

Supplies:

- Wrapped gifts

Water Skiing

I was lucky enough to have grown up with a boat and it only took me one try to stand up and ski. I remember the night beforehand we had watched *The Creature from the Black Lagoon* in 3-D. My dad picked up the glasses at the grocery store and it was a big family event. We were on vacation at a lake house, going out on the lake the following morning, and nobody had the foresight to realize what a bad idea it was for young children to watch a 3-D scary movie about a water monster the night before they were learning to ski.

The next morning, the boat could not have taken off any sooner than it did. My dad's friend was telling me to keep the skis together and bend my knees, and blah, blah, blah. All I could think of was the creature that was about to pull me under and drag me to the bottom of the lake. When I nodded my head that I was ready, the boat roared forward and I stood up. I never wanted to be back in the water again.

You might be asking yourself, "What does this random story have to do with my elf?" I'm glad you asked. Use it as inspiration to make your elf some skis today. We're going to use them twice. Once for water skiing and once for snow skiing. I used the top of a gift box by drawing the outlines of the skis and cutting them out. The outlines should be long, thin rectangles with pointed ends to be curled up once they are cut. I also used blue tissue paper as water and hung a piece of yellow and orange in the background. I created the ski rope with yarn and a pencil.

Supplies:

- Toy boat
- Yarn
- Pencil
- Tissue paper
- Poster board or cardboard (shirt or shoe box works fine)

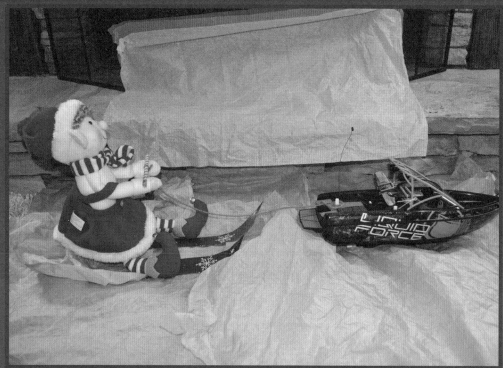

Mummy Is Tired

If this is one of those nights where you just don't have it in you to create elf magic, grab a roll of toilet paper and wrap it around the elf. I felt like this was too easy, so I printed out a picture of ancient Egyptian hieroglyphics to place in the background for added effect. If you're cheap like me, you'll roll the toilet paper back on the roll the following day. Or make the kids do it. Tell them it's a fun game!

Supplies:

- Toilet paper

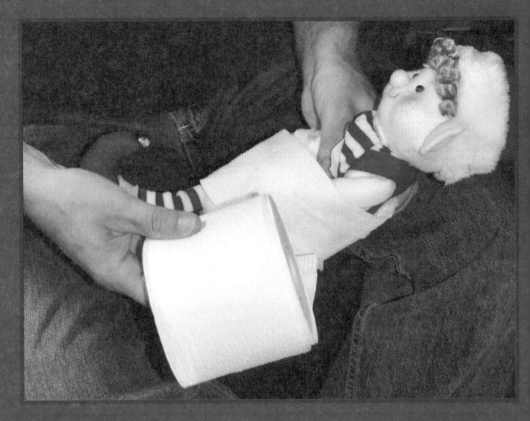

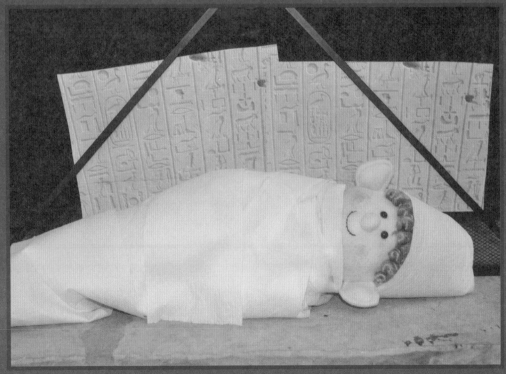

Rub-a-Dub-Dub

This one took a while and I learned a lot about what NOT to do. Don't blow up balloons in the room next to where your children are sleeping. I think I may have developed super lung powers when I had to blow up the raft, after forgetting to do it during the day with an air compressor. I could have sworn I did not overfill the balloons, but at least seven of them popped as I blew.

So, blow up all your balloons ahead of time and store them in large trash bags. You can use the leftovers for later projects. If you go to a party store, you can buy an entire bag of blue balloons. I had originally bought a bag of assorted balloons at the grocery store, and the bag only had six blue ones. (Really? Six?)

Also, if you saved all your paper airplanes, now is the time they will come in handy. First of all, I made sure the tub was dry. Next, I blew up balloons with my super human lungs. I filled the bottom of the tub with a layer of balloons and then added a second layer. Next, I placed the elves in the tub and dumped in all of my balled-up paper airplanes to look like bubbles. I also found a rubber duck and threw it in as well. Rub-a-dub-dub!

Supplies:

- Blue balloons
- Copy paper

Silly

This is how I used the leftover assortment of balloons. This one was a surprise afternoon visit. The kids went out to the play set in the backyard and when they came back in, the elves had been by for a visit.

Supplies:

- Balloons

Snowball Fight I

This one took an hour or so, but can be done in a much simpler way. I think I heard "Have Yourself a Merry Little Christmas" on the way home or had one too many cups of eggnog, because I was feeling good and in the spirit. This was my masterpiece.

I took all the cushions off the couch and placed them in a central area to create a hilly landscape. I had plastic sheeting for painting in the garage, so I cut a piece to drape over the cushions to create the illusion of snow (remember, through the eyes of a child). Next, I took approximately one hundred pieces of copy paper, balled them up and placed them all over the room. Additionally, I raided the shredder from work for a few weeks and collected the paper in large garbage bags, which I hid in my car. As a final touch, I dumped all the shredded paper on top of my creation. A winter wonderland! It was one heck of a snowball fight.

You can do this without the couch cushions or the plastic sheeting,

and definitely without the shredded paper. I wouldn't want anybody to find themselves or their significant other on the naughty list for making a mess. Set the elf and her friends up across the room from each other. Put at least one obstacle in between them and ball up copy paper and place around the scene.

Supplies:

- Copy paper
- Plastic sheeting (optional)
- Shredded paper (optional)

Word Games/Board Games

I had fun with this one; it was a challenging test that only enhanced my word game skills. At least that's what I told myself after spending nearly thirty minutes locked in our guest room trying to fill a board with Christmas words. I should have used Candy Land or Chutes and Ladders!

This one is simple and can take less than two minutes, unless you get overzealous like I did. Set the elf and friends around a board game. Set up any board game and scatter some pieces around as if they they are playing and *bam*—done.

If your children are of reading age and you have a Scrabble board, I am including a picture of the words I came up with. I hope you'll be impressed. Mrs. Deas was not and I'm still looking for a little recognition.

Mrs. Deas would have been more impressed if the elf had folded the laundry.

Supplies:

- Any board game will work

Camp Fire

I once fell in to a campfire. My flip-flop decided to break as I was carrying a load of wood toward the fire. Not wanting to go in face first or to plant my hand in the bottom of the fire to break my fall I turned in mid-air and rolled. I have to say, it may have been the world's greatest evasive action roll—and I have some cool scars to prove it. Needless to say, I have a healthy respect for fire.

I collected a few sticks from the yard and used warm-colored tissue paper to create the fire. I balled up some red, yellow, and orange at the bottom and began placing sticks across. I sat some friends around the fire and even brought out the marshmallows again.

Supplies:

- Sticks
- Tissue paper (warm colors)
- Marshmallows

Rappelling

This is a hobby for people who like to see their lives flash before their eyes. What is wrong with you people? Why would you want to climb down rocks and steep cliffs? If I want a rush, I'll leave for work ten minutes late and try to get there on time. That's a rush!

I tied a piece of yarn to something high and something low, making sure it was nice and tight. I attached the elf by wrapping her arms around the yarn. You can also attach the elf with small pieces of pipe cleaners. As I finished I thought about all the people who do this for fun and smiled.

Supplies:

- Yarn, rope, or string

Story Time

This is another easy one. Place your elf in a seat or on the floor with a book. The hardest part is getting the book to stay in the elf's lap to look like he or she is reading. Place a bunch of stuffed animals around as if they are listening to the story and head off to bed.

Supplies:

- Book
- Stuffed animals

Telescope Blues

My father-in-law bought my children a telescope a few years ago and he failed to tell me I needed a degree from NASA to operate it. They look so simple . . . and hopefully this project will be less problematic.

Just take your elf and your telescope and point it at the sky. If you don't have a telescope, you can roll up a piece of poster board or even a piece of regular size copy paper to fashion one. If you want to get extra credit, cut out a few stars, tape them to the window or wall, and put some space toys around.

Supplies:

- Telescope
- Space toys (optional)

Sack Race

Did you know there is an International Sack Racing Federation? Well, there is. I did some research for this entry. Apparently, sack racing is considered by some people to be a serious sport. Some sources even claim it was an event in the 1904 Olympics. I can't confirm that to be true, but I can confirm that it's a fun scenario for your elf.

All you need for this one are some stuffed animal friends and some paper lunch bags. If you want to get crazy, make a finish line with some streamer or yarn.

Supplies:

- Brown paper bags
- Streamer
- Yarn or streamers for finish line (optional)

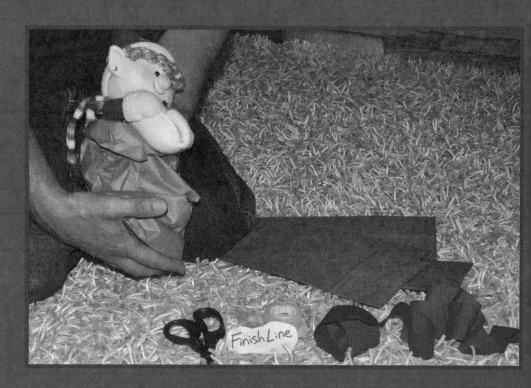

Finish Line

Finish

Dress-Up

I would bet you have some doll clothes or a shirt from one of the kid's teddy bears you can put on the elf. Don't forget to accessorize with whatever you can find—sunglasses, hats, and shoes would make a good start. To add another element of humor, position some dolls around as if they were responsible for the makeover.

Supplies:

- Doll clothes
- Accessories, i.e., sunglasses, hat, or shoes (optional)
- Dolls (optional)

Snowflakes

If the kids have become used to running into the living room to see what the elves have done, this will also keep them on their toes if you set it up in your kitchen, dining room, or in any other room in your house.

All you need is a bunch of ear cleaners or cotton swabs and some imagination.

Supplies:

- Cotton swabs

On Your Mark, Get Set, Go!

This scenario is easy and will take you less than five minutes to set up. I'm sure your garage is full of scooters, bikes, Big Wheels, and other vehicles your children ride around on. A wagon would work just fine. Bring your vehicle(s) of choice into the house. I just happened to have some traffic cones in the garage—not sure why I have them or where they came from. I tell Mrs. Deas that this is why I keep the stuff—you never know when you are going to need it.

I set the cones in a circle and situated the scooters as if the elves and friends were racing. It's as simple as that.

Supplies:

- Toy vehicles
- Cones (optional)

Tangled Up in Lights

Do you have some extra Christmas lights? Of course you do. I'm not sure how it happens, but the lights always manage to magically get tangled, even after you carefully wrap them up and store them. It's kind of like the disappearing sock in the dryer—oh, the mysteries of life.

Supplies:

- Christmas lights

Monster Truck

Luckily, I live in the boonies and don't have to deal with much traffic, but if I did I would have to drive a monster truck. Sometimes, on the way home, I get stuck behind a tractor. Once I even had to wait while a cow made her way across the street. I have a lot of patience, but put me behind the wheel and that all goes out the window.

I didn't have a monster truck toy, so I used a dump truck instead. Sometimes you have to improvise. I placed cushions all over the floor at odd angles and threw a sheet over it to look like a rough course. I also placed rocks on the sheet. I put the elf in the dump truck and hoped my kids' imaginations would take care of the rest.

Supplies:

- Toy truck
- Sheets and cushions/pillows
- Rocks (optional)

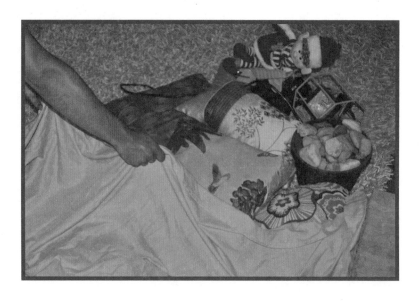

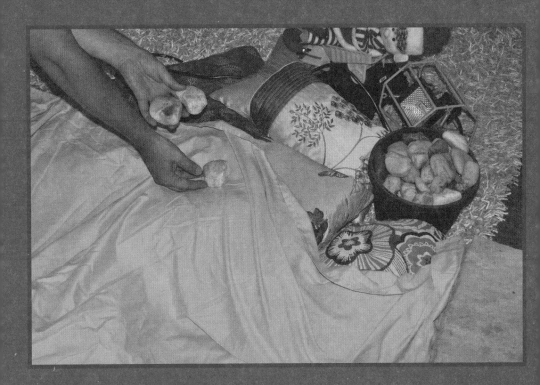

Kite Caper

This is my experience with kites. I end up running around like a fool trying to get the kites off the ground. If they ever do get off the ground, they immediately get stuck in a tree and all the string gets tangled into the world's most amazing knot. I'm not a big fan of kites.

You can use a real kite for this or easily create one with construction paper and yarn. Cut out a big diamond, poke a hole in the bottom, and attach a piece of yarn. I attached mine to the Christmas tree with tape.

Supplies:

- Kite or construction paper
- Yarn or string
- Tape

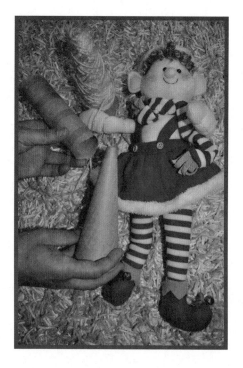

Dishwasher Bath

This is a quick and easy setup. The only hard part is making sure the dishwasher is empty, which at our house is almost never. It's kind of like the trash can—always full. Grab a bottle of shampoo, a bar of soap, and any other items you keep around your tub or shower. A shower cap makes a nice addition. Got a loofah? Use that too. I put our elf on the top rack and left it open. Then I placed the bathing items around and left the rest to my kids' imaginations. You can always leave the dishwasher closed if you want to add a game of hide-and-seek to your morning.

Supplies:

- Bathing items and various toiletries (shampoo, soap, loofah, etc.)

Dominoes

Does anyone actually know the rules for dominoes? I have owned this game my entire life and—until this project—I haven't once wondered how to actually play. All I've ever done is set them up and knocked them down. I would be willing to bet I'm not the only one who owns dominoes and doesn't know how to play.

Supplies:

* Dominoes

Bottom of the Drawer

Have you ever lost something and looked around the house feverishly for it? Of course you have. We seem to do this a couple times a week at my house.

This setup is in honor of our frantic searches and the treasures at the bottom of drawers. Unlike my expeditions for lost items, which have taken whole afternoons, this only takes about thirty seconds. Open a drawer, any drawer, and stuff as much of your elf in as possible, leaving one or both feet hanging out.

Supplies:

- No supplies needed

Trapped

As I was putting away one of the Christmas boxes in the garage, I saw the pet carrier and thought it would be pretty cool if all our stuffed animals caught our elf in the carrier. I snuck all the stuffed animals out of my kids' rooms and placed them around the pet carrier with the elf trapped inside. And the tables were turned!

Supplies:

- Pet carrier
- Stuffed animals

Tennis, Anyone?

My family loves tennis, especially my mom. We played as a family growing up and I have to say I was pretty good. I did, however, have a little too much baseball in my swing, but I learned to control it most of the time. Every now and then I hit a ball over the fence. A tennis home run!

For this setup I used tennis rackets, some tennis balls, and one couch cushion as the net. I threw a Christmas quilt over the cushions because I had no idea how shabby they looked until I pulled them off the couch. If you only have one elf, it's time to get out the stuffed animals again. Set them around with rackets, balls, and add a few action poses that would make Jimmy Connors proud.

Supplies:

- Tennis rackets and balls
- Couch cushions

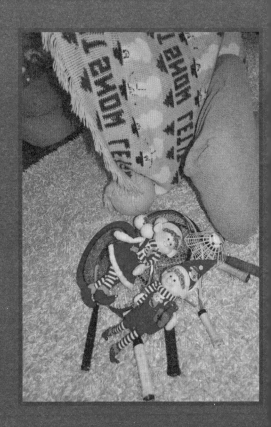

Dr. Elf

I hope you are a little more organized than I am when it comes to first aid. We don't even have a first aid kit, and our medicines and supplies are scattered in cabinets and cupboards throughout the house. Place your elf as if he is examining a stuffed animal friend. I used a doll for this one. As I was searching through drawers, the pantry, and under sinks, I even found a stethoscope. Where did that come from?

Supplies:

- First aid items such as bandages, gauze, thermometer, etc.

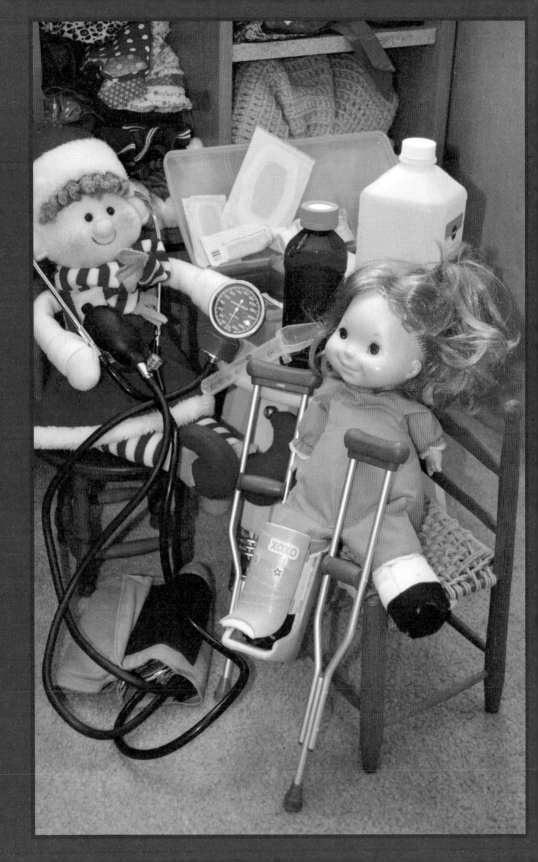

Piggy Bank Deposit

When my daughter was born, we decided to start collecting piggy banks for her. When the collection reached nearly fifteen piggy banks, we ran out of room for them and decided we were going to stop. We should have collected thimbles or something smaller.

I used one of her many piggy banks for this one and set it up as though the elf was caught in the act of giving her a dollar. If you want to be a big spender, use a twenty-dollar bill.

Supplies:

- Piggy bank
- Dollar bill

Fort Night

Who didn't make forts out of the couch cushions as kids? I know I did—and thanks to our elf, I got the chance to do it again. So gather all the pillows, the couch cushions, quilts and blankets, and channel your inner child to create something exciting.

You can also use chairs instead of couch cushions. Turn four chairs backwards, making a large square, and throw a sheet or some large blankets over it. Young kids will not only love the setup, but will probably play inside the fort all day.

Supplies:

- Couch cushions
- Sheet or quilt

Poker Night

All you need for this one is a deck of cards and something to use as poker chips. This is another instance, like with dominoes, where I have no idea of the rules. I know most grown men would never admit that, but I hate losing money and subsequently never had the desire to learn. I went to Las Vegas once and spent forty dollars, and felt terrible about it. If I want to play the odds, I'll take a gamble that Mrs. Deas really meant it when she said not to get her a gift this year.

Supplies:

- Playing cards
- Poker chips or substitute with something like peppermints

Parachute

To create the illusion of our elf parachuting into the living room, I started with our coat rack. If you do not have a coat rack, you might use a pot rack, ceiling fan, stocking holder, string over a balcony or loft, etc. I also used some blue streamers, a plastic grocery bag, and I cut out two clouds with white copy paper. You will also need a fan or two.

The elf I used for this one is wearing a scarf, so I used it to attach him to the coat rack. I slipped a plastic grocery bag over his arms and used a clip to keep his hands together. Then I cut small pieces of streamer and taped them to the coat rack (shorter pieces work better). Next, I cut two curvy lines around white copy paper and taped the clouds near the top of the coat rack. I started with one fan, which works fine, but added a second to further animate the streamers and parachute.

Supplies:

- Plastic grocery bags
- Blue streamer
- Tape
- Fan
- Copy paper
- Hat/coat rack or somewhere to suspend elf

Follow the Yarn

For as simple as this one is, the kids thought it was a blast. It seemed as if I used nearly seven miles of yarn. I started at the top of the stairs and went downstairs, around tables, over and around chairs, among other furniture. At this point, I was getting pretty dizzy. The yarn finally ended in the guest bedroom behind some pillows. Like a pot of gold at the end of a rainbow a treasure was waiting—the elf!

Supplies:

- Yarn

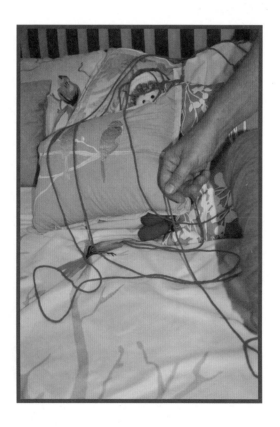

Tug-of-War

The culmination of elementary school field day back in my day was always the tug-of-war. It didn't matter if your team had won every other event, it didn't mean diddly squat unless you won the end-of-the-day tug-of-war. At my school, it was like a death match.

With cheerful memories in mind, I set up a little tug-of-war match with my elf and some of the other stuffed animals. In my basement, I just happened to have a thick rope like the one we used to use in the tug-of-war. Assuming you don't have one, you can use any type of rope, yarn, or even string.

Supplies:

- Rope, string, or yarn
- Bandana or scarf

Roller Rink

Sticking with elementary school memories, I don't think I'll ever forget the roller rink. Once a month, our school took over the rink on Friday night, and their disco ball and couples-skates still live in my memory.

So, in honor of the roller rink, put your elf in roller skates or roller blades, if you have them. To spice it up, you can hang some streamers from the ceiling fan or put some balloons around the room, or both.

Supplies:

- Roller skates or blades
- Streamer
- Balloons

Let's Build Something

Gather up some tools and look for something around the garage or basement that the elf could be building or fixing. I found a birdhouse. I told the kids it had been broken and the elf repaired it. They were impressed.

I grabbed a few tools out of my tool bag and some scrap wood from the basement and placed it around the elf as if he had rebuilt the birdhouse. After taking the picture, I found some other things I had set out for myself the day before and had forgotten. I had a box of nails and some work goggles that would've looked really cute on one of the elves, which didn't make it into the picture. Feel free to use these suggestions for your scene.

Supplies:

- Random tools
- An item for the elf to fix or build

Do You Copy?

Okay, I'll admit I've actually photocopied my face in a copier. Don't lie. I'll bet you have at least thought about doing it, too.

Most home printers have a copier and this idea only takes a few minutes. Place your elf under the copier and make a few copies with different poses. Place the copies next to the machine and leave the last one in the tray with your elf under the copier's hood.

Make sure you hide or throw away the one you made of yourself!

Supplies:

- Copier
- A few scanned copies of the elf

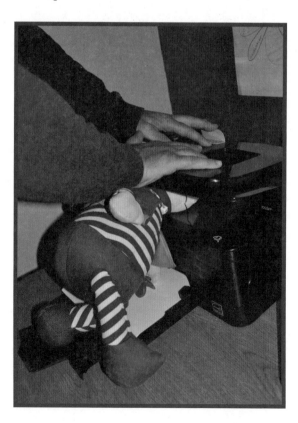

Fruit Basket Turnover

Why can't bananas taste like potato chips and oranges taste like peanut butter cups? Why can't broccoli taste like donuts and baked chicken like prime rib? We have a big fruit bowl at home, which I avoid at all cost, but it did finally come in handy as I buried the elf in it with his feet sticking out. I'm sure he will be as disappointed as I was that pears don't taste like cotton candy.

Supplies:

- Bowl of fruit

Tower Power

Get every cushion in the house and see how high you can stack them. Consider it a game. Of course start with the big ones on bottom and save the smaller, softer ones for the top. I was hoping to reach the ceiling, but I didn't have enough cushions to quite make it to my goal. Pretend that you are playing with giant building blocks. Have fun!

Note: Keep away from fragile furniture to avoid the tower falling and breaking any of your belongings.

Supplies:

- Couch cushions and pillows

Ice Skating

Find some kind of large container that you can fit in your freezer to create a large piece of ice. If you live in a cold climate, you have the option of setting it outside. I found what I think is called a dishpan. I filled it with about two inches of water and put it in the freezer for an entire day.

Just before the kids got up, I popped it out of the pan and placed it in the sink. I put the elf in a pair of ice skates. For those of you who do not have skates in the house, you can also make a homemade pair using various

household items. I used duct tape, folded to look like a blade to the bottom of a piece of fabric. You could even use a shoe with a piece of folded tape attached to the bottom. Use your imagination.

Supplies:

- Ice skates or shoe
- Dish pan, pot or tin
- Freezer
- Ice

Giddy Up, Cowgirl

I had to borrow a pair of cowboy boots for this setup. If you have toy horses or cows, or anything you might find on a ranch, get them out and set up your scene. I even added a lasso because I have too much free time.

Supplies:

- Cowgirl hat and boots
- Yarn
- Stuffed horse and/or cow

The Big Catch

I don't do a lot of fishing. Every time I go, I seem to catch myself, one of my friends, or a tree limb. To avoid injury, I used a pipe cleaner as the hook, and attached it to a piece of wire and a stick I found in the yard. Lots of snacks and candies come in fish shapes. You can arrange them on a piece of paper cut with a curved edge to look like water or, if they won't dissolve in water, you can use a bowl like I did in my photo.

Just for old time's sake, I accidentally poked myself with the sharp piece of metal inside the pipe cleaner. Ouch!

Supplies:

- Stick or similar item to use as pole
- Wire, string, or yarn
- Pipe cleaner
- Fish-shaped candy or snack item
- Cut blue paper to resemble water or a bowl of water

Boat for Sail

This setup takes a little skill if you have a big stuffed elf like ours. If you have a little skinny elf, you should have no problems. I'm sure you have something that floats. If you have a boat, perfect. If you don't, don't worry; you can use a plastic container as a substitute.

I used a remote control boat and had to tape it to the side of the bathtub in a dry spot using painter's tape. If I didn't, the boat would float away and the elf would get wet. If you don't have any kind of boat, you can use a plastic food container. We have them in all sizes. I've included one in my photo along with my boat so you can see the two methods.

Supplies:

- Toy boat or plastic container
- Painter's tape

Trapped in a Vase

It doesn't get much easier than this. Stick your elf's head down in a vase, add some flowers (we had fake ones), and call it a night.

Supplies:

- Vase
- Flowers (real or fake optional)

Kiss the Cook

This setup can be as easy or complicated as you make it. A frying pan, spatula, and a fried egg impressed my kids. You could have your elf sitting next to the mixer ready to make pancakes or making toast with the butter dish and a knife by their side.

Supplies:

- Cooking items such as pots, pans, spatula, spices, etc.

Surfing the Web

I'm fairly certain my kids know more about computers than I do. I went to college in 1991 and nobody had a computer.

For this one, I put a tech savvy elf in front of the computer looking at a picture of Santa. I hope the kids don't ever search the Internet to find out if Santa is real. Unplug! Unplug!

Supplies:

- Computer
- Christmas-themed image (Stored on computer or searched on the internet)

Building Blocks

I will admit I had to look this one up on the Internet. I searched "building block Christmas tree" and got a good idea of what I was looking for. I did my best and the kids thought it was great. The children had used all the green blocks so I had to make my tree with red. I will admit I felt proud and then hurt when the kids tore my creation apart.

Supplies:

- Any variety of building blocks

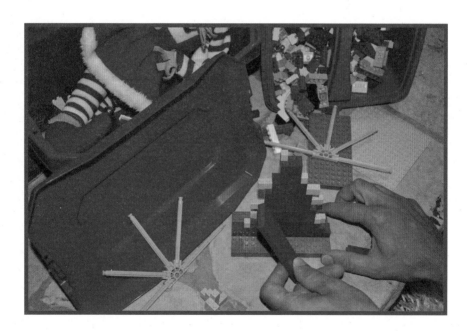

Puzzles Are Cool

Call me an old man if you'd like, but I like putting puzzles together. I'm not sure why it's fun for me, but it is.

In my house, we have boxes and boxes of puzzles. I'm sure they're all missing at least one piece, but it didn't matter for this one. Get a puzzle with twenty-five or fifty pieces, or if you are really tired, get one of the wooden ones with less than fifteen. Put a quarter of the pieces together and scatter the rest around the elf and go get yourself some shut-eye.

Supplies:

- Puzzle

Snowball Fight II

My first snowball fight was elaborate. I'll admit I was showing off. This one is easy and took less than ten minutes to setup. I placed the elf on one side of the kitchen table and a stuffed penguin on the other. I turned two small dishes over in front of them and covered them and the area in front with white tissue paper. On the dishes, I used large marshmallows to create a snow fort wall. Then, I used smaller marshmallows to represent the snowballs and randomly placed them all over the scene.

Supplies:

- Marshmallows (large and small)
- Tissue paper

Black Diamonds

Remember when we made water skis? I hope you saved them because we are going to use them again. I used pencils for ski poles and pipe cleaners to attach them to the elf's hands. If you saved your pieces of balled up white copy paper, use them again as snow. I used white tissue paper. I threw a blanket with snowflakes over the ironing board as my base. For the moguls, I draped a small white baby blanket over some small plastic cups. If you look closely enough at the picture, you can see how I stood my elf on a cardboard roll and even tied her to the snowman behind her to make her stand.

Supplies:

- Copy paper
- Tissue paper
- Poster board or cardboard (shirt box or shoe box works fine)
- Pencils or similar item for poles

Slurp, Slurp, Slurp

Elves love sugar, and so do I. Recently, Mrs. Deas put us both on a diet and she somehow made the authoritarian decision that we would not have a "cheat" meal for three weeks. I'm not sure how she came up with this figure, but sometimes you don't question Mrs. Deas.

Don't worry, though; your elf has a digestive system perfect for handling sugar and all kinds of other delicious sugary snacks. Put a straw in a bottle of syrup or jelly and put the straw in the elf's mouth and *bam*, done. Go to bed, and learn from me—don't eat four donuts and three pieces of cake— it's not as fun as it sounds.

Supplies:

- Syrup, jelly, honey, or a bag of sugar
- Straw

Little Drummer Girl

Here's a chance to make your elf musical. I created a drum set with plastic containers. You can use cans, pot and pans, and anything remotely resembling a drum.

Supplies:

- Plastic containers, pots, pans, etc.
- Pipe cleaners
- Small wooden dowels or similar for drum sticks

Winter Dress

Dress your elf up with winter mittens, scarves, hats, etc. Make it look like she is about to go outside or just came back in from the cold. And don't worry, as soon as you get the elf dressed, she won't tell you that all your work was in vain because she has to go to the bathroom. We'll leave that to your children.

Supplies:

- Winter clothes such as hats, scarves, or mittens

Tea Party

If you have little girls at home, I would bet you have a miniature tea set around somewhere. However, if you don't, you can use regular tea or coffee cups, saucers (or small plates, as I like to call them), and spoons. Set some tea bags around, sugar packets, and of course invite some friends for a spot of tea.

Supplies:

- Saucers and tea cups
- Tea bags, sugar packets
- Spoons

Color Me Confused

I'm sure your kids have a million coloring books. Get out the crayons or markers and color half of one page, as if the elf did it, and prop her up next to the open book with crayons scattered around. If you end up coloring the whole page, start a new one and order yourself one of those adult coloring books tomorrow.

Supplies:

- Crayons, markers, or color pencils
- Coloring book

Hiding in Stuffed Animals

I'm not sure how it happened, but we've somehow accumulated eighty-three stuffed animals. Yes, I counted. And those are just the ones we still have. Many more have come and gone. Hopefully you'll have enough for these easy scene. Make a pile of your stuffed animals and hide your elf in them!

Supplies:

- Stuffed animals

Race Day

I set this one up just like the sack race. I used the same finish line and everything. Instead of brown paper sacks, I found vehicles for the stuffed animals. Simple. Just make sure the elf is winning! Elves rule.

Supplies:

- Toy vehicles
- Streamer

It's Frosty in Here

If you live somewhere where there's snow on the ground this one is easy. Make a tiny snowman. If you only see snow one or two days a year or never where you live, this one can be challenging. I certainly didn't want to build another marshmallow snowman since we've done that project already. I considered making one with crushed ice. I pondered and contemplated and nearly hurt myself thinking so much about it. I finally took the easy way out and used one of our snowman decorations. I put a Popsicle in his hands and called it a night. If you make one out of snow, shaved ice, ice cubes, or something else your brain crafts—you got me beat on this one.

Supplies:

- Plush snowman or snowman decoration

Spare Me

Bowling is one of those things that looks so easy, but isn't.

The bowling alley gave one of my kids a bowling pin for having a birthday party at the local bowling alley. I placed this on one side of the lane and a bowling ball I borrowed on the other. I arranged plastic cups as pins and used a white basketball for the elf's bowling ball. Then I added buffalo snow on the side of a carpet runner to look like the alley. Not only was this an easy setup, the kids had fun playing with it for an hour or so.

Supplies:

- Ball
- Cups
- Buffalo snow (optional)

Hide-and-Seek

This one involves many stuffed animals—the more, the better. If your children have to go to school, or you have to rush them off in the morning somewhere, you probably want to save this one for the weekend. My picture only shows a small part of this, but I had stuffed animals hidden all over the house. I think I hid approximately forty of them. I tried to make it look like the elf was the one counting. You can put a blindfold on the one counting, turn them against the wall, or put their face down in a pillow.

Supplies:

- Stuffed animals

Flying High

I used a piece of poster board to make the airplane. The folds were a little harder to make with poster board, but the final product still resembled an airplane. I stapled the bottom so it would all hold together, then poked a few holes in various places and tied it to the ceiling fan. Finally, I placed buffalo snow on top of the fan blades to look like clouds. If you have time, you might add designs to the poster board but I'd had a long day and left it plain. You might even use a toy airplane or helicopter, if you have one.

Supplies:

- Poster board (or any variety of flying toy)
- Yarn
- Staples
- Buffalo snow (optional)

Put a Lid on It

This is another one where you'll need to sneak a lot of stuffed animals out of the kids' rooms. You're probably getting pretty good at this by now. The more you can get, the better. Also, you'll need lots of hats. Baseball caps, cowboy hats, winter hats, rain hats, bike helmets, etc. The more variety you have for this one the better. You can set this one up like a party, put the stuffed animals all in a circle, have them playing follow the leader, or just set them all over the room.

Supplies:

- Assortment of hats
- Stuffed animals

She Shoots, She Scores!

Set up a goal and find a stuffed animal to be a goaltender. The elf can be the one about to score and have some stuffed animal friends around. Easy.

Supplies:

- Soccer ball
- Cushions
- Blanket, quilt, or sheet
- Stuffed animal (goaltender)

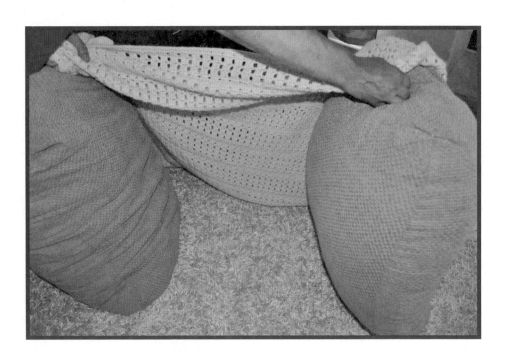

Clumsy Elf

Everyone is clumsy, including elves! Take your most uncoordinated elf and wrap him in string, rope, or ribbon and hang him from the tree or wherever else he may have been up to mischief.

Supplies:

- Rubber bands

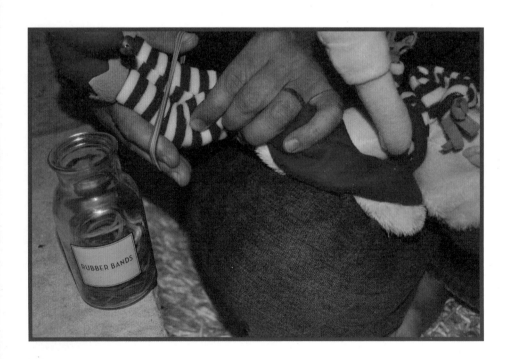

Pumping Iron

I'm sure you, too, have some useless workout equipment somewhere in your living space. Or maybe you actually use yours—good for you. Set up your elf as if he has been pumping iron all night. If you don't have any workout equipment (I applaud you for not pretending to exercise like me), you can make a simple barbell with marshmallows and toothpicks. You can make the elf look like he's bench-pressing by attaching the marshmallows with something longer like a skewer or a pencil. I also scattered some of my other exercise equipment around the room so the kids would make the connection.

After moving all that stuff upstairs, I felt so good I think I'm going to start working out tomorrow. Just kidding!

Supplies:

- Exercise equipment
- Marshmallows
- Pencil, skewer, or stick

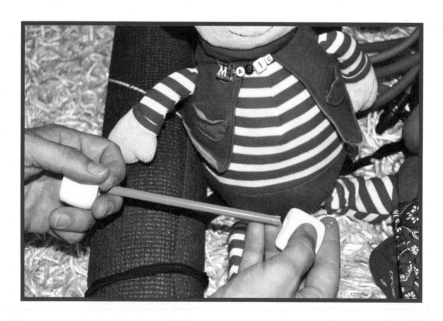

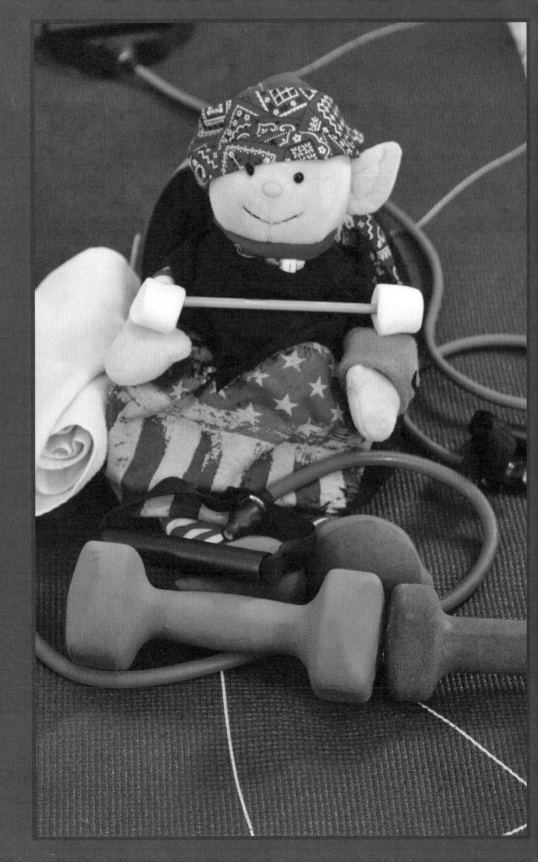

Game On

I'm sure most households have some sort of gaming system, so this setup will be relatively easy. Put the elf in a chair in front of the television with the controller and a few games stacked around. If you have time before the kids wake up, turn it on. Game on!

Supplies:

- Video game console and controller
- Games

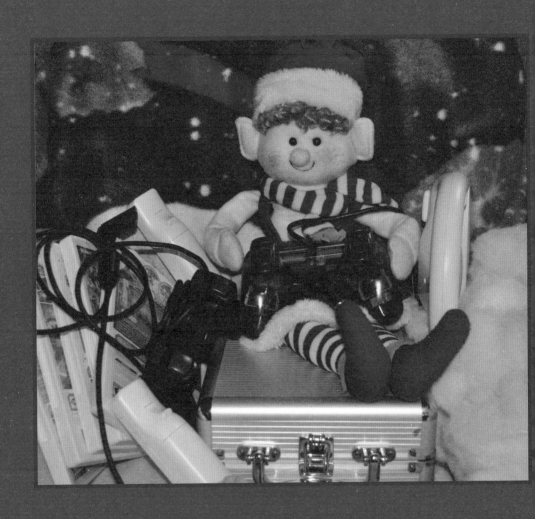

Shredding the Slopes

All I know about snowboarding is what I've seen on television and what I hear about from my younger brother. I've come to the conclusion that snowboarding is like skateboarding on snow. It's for the young and the cool. I am neither of those things.

It just so happens one of our dolls is so cool that she has a snowboard. So, I used it for my setup. If you don't have a cool doll at your house with a hip snowboard, you can easily fashion one out of a piece of cardboard. Use a scrap piece of wood or even something like a remote control turned upside down. I used a remote in my picture alongside my cool doll's snowboard so you can see how the not-so-cool among us do it.

Supplies:

- Tissue paper
- Copy paper
- Remote control or similar item to represent snowboard

Slam Dunk

I made a basket by cutting out the middle of a paper plate and taping white streamers to the inside. I stacked a few basketballs and even snuck a basketball trophy out of my son's room.

Supplies:

- Paper plate
- White streamer
- Tape
- Basketball
- Trophy (optional)

Fold It Up

If you have an ironing board, iron, laundry basket, or a pile of unfolded clothes, use them for this scene. A few shirts the elf has ironed on hangers make a nice touch.

Supplies:

- Ironing board
- Laundry basket
- Hangers
- Pile of unfolded clothes

Wrap It Up

I hope I was able to give you a lot of good ideas and most importantly decrease your stress about having an elf, so you can have fun with it. We allow our elves to stay until New Year's Day, but after Christmas they don't "move" on their own, they just hang out and rest after a busy season of toy making. The kids put them in their rooms, sleep with them, whatever—like I said, our elves are pretty laid back and don't have too many rules except to have fun and make memories.

If your kids are like mine, they might throw you a curve ball with the elves and start leaving out snacks or writing letters to them every night and expecting a response. When these unexpected things happen, we figure out ways that don't take away from the fun.

As the letter writing intensified last year, Mrs. Deas finally had to deliver a letter from Santa, which said the elves were getting too busy to answer any more letters. Our elf had fallen behind making trains and needed to work so all the good boys and girls would get their toys.

When the kids started feeding the elves oranges and crackers every night, we had to tell them that elves liked to peel their own oranges; we were tired of wasting oranges and crackers.

Thanks for reading, and again, Merry Christmas!

For this last one, Mrs. Deas always laughs at the way I wrap gifts. I wrap gifts as poorly as I make snowmen out of marshmallows. So, in honor of Mrs. Deas and all her help, this one is for her!

Supplies:

- Wrapping paper
- Scissors